LULU
AND
THE CASTLE OF SLEEP

DEBBIE WHITE

Illustrated by Judy Brown

PACIFIC
LEARNING

© 2001 Pacific Learning
© 2000 Written by **Debbie White**
Illustrated by **Judy Brown**
US Edit by **Alison Auch**

This Americanized Edition of *Luke Lively and the Castle
of Sleep*, originally published in English in 2000, is
published by arrangement with Oxford University
Press.

05 04 03 02 01
10 9 8 7 6 5 4 3 2 1

Published by
Pacific Learning
P.O. Box 2723
Huntington Beach, CA 92647-0723
www.pacificlearning.com

ISBN: 1-59055-048-X
PL-7500

Contents

1

The Next Best Thing

It was just after lunch at the Ministry for Fairy-tale Regeneration (M.F.R. for short), and the Chief Computer Officer, Ron Smallweed, was about to make a horrible discovery.

He had asked Fickle Finger, the M.F.R.'s awesomely powerful computer, to access the Sleeping Beauty File, and before he could say "Witches' Whiskers," it was on-screen. All the Sleeping Beauties that had ever existed scrolled past, neatly listed in date order. The last Sleeping Beauty on the list was Aurora Rose Rams-Botham, born June 1891 at Cutforth Castle, into a family with royal connections, but absolutely no cash.

At that moment, she was still snoring away happily in a forgotten room, in the tallest turret of Cutforth Castle. She was scheduled to be woken up tomorrow by dark and handsome Prince Hugo. Hugo, however, had other ideas. He was already madly in love with his Personal Fitness Trainer, Paula. He planned to live happily ever after with her instead.

In fact, they were just about to run off together and elope.

"They can't," shouted Jackson Bigwood, Minister in Charge at the M.F.R. "That's not allowed. Are you sure Fickle Finger is right?"

"Fickle doesn't make mistakes," said Ron, looking hurt.

"In that case," said the Minister, "we'll have to find someone else – fast. Ask Fickle for a list of other suitable princes."

Quick as a flash, Ron typed in the request and grabbed the list off the printer. He looked at it. Then he flipped it over.

"There's nothing on it," he wailed. "It's completely blank."

"Give it to me," said the Minister crossly. "Let me take a look."

Even with his reading glasses on, he could see that Ron was right.

"What does it mean?" asked Ron.

"It means," said the Minister, "that we've run out of princes."

"What are we going to do?"

"Ask Fickle for a list of the NEXT BEST THING."

Ron looked blank.

"Look," said the Minister slowly. "Suppose Prince Hugo's great-grandfather –"

"King Havelock," interrupted Ron.

"– hadn't actually married Prince Hugo's great-grandmother, Queen Hilda."

"But he did," said Ron. "People said it was the fairy-tale wedding of the century."

"Yes I know that," said the Minister, who was starting to sound grumpy. "Just suppose he hadn't. What if he'd never married at all? Who would have been the next person in line for the throne?"

"Um," said Ron, hazarding a guess. "One of King Havelock's nieces or nephews?"

"He didn't have any. Unfortunately, he was an only child."

"In that case," said Ron, "we had better ask Fickle."

They turned to look at the screen. Fickle, using its awesomely powerful artificial intelligence, had already come up with an answer.

"Luke Lively?" said the Minister. "What kind of stupid name is that? Who is he? Where does he live? What does he look like? Where does he go to school?"

"Hold on," said Ron, his fingers flying over the keyboard. "I can't type that fast."

"Oh!" gasped the Minister as the answers popped up. "There must be a mistake."

Ron was about to say, "Fickle doesn't..." but the words stuck in his throat.

Fickle had downloaded Luke's school picture, which was very unfair. With his hair wetted down and parted in the middle, his pimply chin, and his immaculately pressed shirt and stupid tie, he looked like an alien from another planet. (Even his mom wouldn't recognize him.)

He read the list of Luke's interests:

Soccer
Computers
Girls...

Then he read the list of Luke's dislikes:

School
Showers
Girls...

He stared at a gruesomely detailed picture of Luke's bedroom at 1223 Willow Street:

Then he thought of Aurora Rose Rams-Botham of Cutforth Castle, who listed her interests as:

Croquet

Sketching

Playing the piano

Taking apart anything
   mechanical

Her dislikes were:

Spiders

Plain yogurt

Governess Wibberley

Not being allowed to take
   things apart

Somehow he just couldn't see it working.

"It was always going to be a tricky one. Even with Prince Hugo," the Minister was saying. "After all, things have changed in the last hundred years or so. Think about all the things we have now that they didn't have then:

"Space Travel."

"Highways."

"Supermarkets."

"Computers."

"Fast food. Microwave ovens. Soft toilet paper," Ron added.

"They are both going to have to make adjustments," continued the Minister. "It's going to be a rough ride. Still, we don't have much choice. If our Sleeping Beauty isn't woken up, the whole cycle goes down the tubes. Kaput! No more Sleeping Beauties ever. Then, before you can say Rumpelstiltskin, the whole Ministry's being downsized and we're out on our ears."

"Eeek!" squeaked Ron.

"Exactly," said the Minister. "So we can't afford to make any mistakes. We need help."

"Anyone in mind?" asked Ron.

"Only the best F.G. in the business," said the Minister.

"Who's that?" said Ron, desperately trying to think of all the Fairy Godmothers he'd ever met.

"Don't you know?" snapped the Minister.

"Is it that short fat one? You know, the one we had to use when we had trouble with Cinderella?"

"No! Don't be silly. It's Gretl Greta, naturally."

"Gretl Greta!" gasped Ron. Of course he had heard of her.

"The only problem is, she's on a climbing trip in the Swiss Alps. I think if we send a quick message on her pager, she'd be back here in no time at all."

"Fantastic!" said Ron.

2

Castle Ahoy

By the time Gretl arrived at the Ministry she was in a very bad mood.

"Okay, Bigwood," she growled. "You've just called me back from the first decent vacation I've had in two hundred years. You'd better have a good explanation."

She banged her hiking boots down on the Minister's desk. As the Minister began to fill Gretl in on all the details, she stopped looking quite so irritated and started to look interested.

"Hmmm," she said. "How extraordinary! What did you say this young man's name was, again? Also, he's had no experience being a prince at all?"

"None whatsoever," said the Minister. "So you can see why we had to call you in."

"Of course," said Gretl. "You did the right thing. Don't worry, Bigwood, Gretl Greta's on the case."

Luke Lively, hanging around the kitchen at 1223 Willow Street, didn't know that Gretl was about to change his life forever, so he was complaining about being bored. It was a tactic he often used on his mom, and it always got excellent results.

"There's nothing to do. I wish something exciting would happen. It's Saturday and you're going to spend all day working. You won't pay any attention to me at all."

"You're right. Nothing exciting is going to happen," said Luke's mom. "Not until I've finished balancing Mr. Boggit's books, at least." (Mrs. Lively was a Certified Public Accountant.) "Why don't you run down to the store for me? We're out of milk."

Luke said nothing.

"Here's some money," said his mom. She knew she was going to be working all day and she felt guilty about it. "You can spend the change on candy."

"Thanks, Mom!" said Luke, giving her a quick hug before rushing out of the back door. "When I come back, I'll be in a good mood. I promise!"

He leaped on the seat of his mountain bike and sped off toward the store.

He'd just made up his mind to buy a bag of super-sour cherries when he realized he was going the wrong way. He was riding down Willow Street and away from the store.

"Jumping junipers!" he muttered and tried to brake. Nothing happened. The bike kept rolling down the hill. At the bottom, it turned left and very soon he was heading out into the countryside.

"Juggling junipers," he shouted as his bike took a sudden turn off the paved road and onto a rutted dirt road.

"H-e-e-e-l-p!" he wailed as the bike headed off across the bumps.

Poor Luke. His legs had been whirling around so fast on the pedals, they felt like jelly. Then, just as he was thinking he couldn't take anymore, the bike suddenly stopped. He somersaulted over the handlebars and rolled into a muddy puddle at the foot of a large oak tree.

"Ha!" said a voice.

Luke looked around. At first he couldn't see anyone. Then a little old lady appeared from behind the tree. She was wearing a wool suit and sensible shoes. "*There* you are," she said. "Not much to look at, are you? You don't even have a decent horse."

She poked Luke's bike with her stick.

Poor Luke. Not much to look at! He couldn't help being a little pimply. Everyone was at his age. Still, that didn't keep him from feeling sensitive about it. Anyway, how dare she poke his bike like that!

He glared at her, but she ignored him. "If you hurry, you'll make it in time. Down the hill and through Dazely Woods – you can't miss it once you hit the old road."

"Miss what?" asked Luke, bewildered.

"Sleeping Beauty's Castle, of course," she said, starting to turn away.

Luke's mouth dropped open. He looked like a beached fish gasping for air.

"Wait a minute," he said. "I thought you said Sleeping Beauty's Castle."

"I did," she said.

She's totally nuts, he thought.

"You don't have a cellular phone, do you?" he asked nervously. "Then I could call my mom and ask her to come and get me."

"Good grief," she snorted. "What next? Jack getting his mom to help him climb the Beanstalk? I ask you."

"Ask me what?" said Luke, bewildered. "Who's Jack?"

She didn't reply. She just strode off. He didn't hear the "bleep, bleep, bleep" as she called the M.F.R. number. "Ron. It's Gretl. He's on track for the castle. Due fourteen hundred hours."

Luke wasn't at all sure what to do next. He could wait and hope someone normal turned up. Or... He sighed and picked up his bike. Sleeping Beauty's Castle. Please. Who did she think he was?

Fifteen minutes later, at two o'clock exactly, Luke arrived at the gates of a very large and imposing castle. He could just see its turrets peeking out from a huge rosebush.

That's funny, he thought. His mom loved visiting old castles – she'd taken him to lots of them – but he didn't remember this one. Never mind, the castle was bound to have a phone. All he had to do was knock on the door and ask if he could call his mom. The only problem was, he could see the castle's massive oak front door, but he couldn't reach it. There were too many thorns.

Then a cheerful thought struck him. If there was a front door, there was bound to be a back door too, wasn't there? Dropping his bike to the ground, he scrambled around to see if he was right.

3

Kiss, Kiss

"He's supposed to hack his way through, not go around to the back!" groaned the Minister. He'd been tracking Luke's progress on Fickle's monitor.

"It doesn't matter," said Ron. "As long as he gets inside, goes up to the tower, and wakes up Aurora Rose with a kiss."

"That's the part I'm really worried about," said the Minister. "Frankly, I just can't see it happening."

"Hello? Anyone at home?"

Luke carefully turned the door handle. He'd had a pretty weird day so far, and he wasn't going to feel safe until he was back home. He stepped inside. So far, so good.

Someone was there too. He could see a woman wearing a white cap and a long dress and apron, sitting in a chair by a huge old cooking range.

Phew! he thought, feeling better. He must be in a living history museum. He'd been to one with his class at school. Actors dressed up and pretended to be people from history. It was pretty cool.

He tiptoed over and touched the woman gently on the shoulder. She stopped snoring, but she didn't wake up, even when he shouted in her ear. *She's probably hard of hearing,* he thought, trying to stay calm. *I'll just have to find someone who isn't.*

He found the servants' staircase tucked away in the far corner of the room.

"If I go up here," he said out loud, trying to sound brave, "I'll probably get to the main part of the castle." He was right.

At first he thought there was no one around. Then he spotted a maid sprawled out fast asleep on the main staircase. A butler, head tipped back and mouth wide open, was sitting on a small, hard chair by the giant oak front door. He was fast asleep too.

Luke could feel his heart doing a tap dance inside his chest. Of course he didn't believe in fairy tales. No one his age did. Still, he was beginning to think that finding a castle covered in roses and full of sleeping people was too much of a coincidence.

He had this feeling that at the very top of the castle, there was going to be a princess fast asleep and waiting for a handsome prince to wake her up.

If there was, it wouldn't do any harm to take a look, would it?

After all, *he* wasn't the handsome prince she'd been waiting for, was he?

"Oh, help," gasped Luke, still a little out of breath from climbing the two hundred stairs to the top of the castle's tallest turret. He hadn't really expected to find a princess, but there she was.

He stood on a stool at the side of an enormous four-poster bed and looked down into the face of the sleeping Aurora Rose. *So this is what Sleeping Beauty looks like,* he thought.

To be honest, he was disappointed. He had expected her to look like a fairy-tale princess. You know, long silky hair, soft downy skin, fragile beauty – that sort of stuff. This girl didn't look fragile at all. In fact, she looked pretty solid. There was something about her strong mouth, the jut of her chin, and the regal outline of her nose that made him feel kind of wimpy and pathetic.

He was beginning to feel deflated, like the last balloon left at the end of the party. Suddenly, he remembered what came next in the story.

"Oh, yuck!" he said, with a shudder. "There's no way I'm going to k..."

Before he had time to finish the sentence, he felt a bony hand grip him by the back of the neck. It was Gretl.

"Give her a kiss, Luke," she said with a steely smile. "If you don't, I'll turn you into a worm."

"What kind of worm?" said Luke, alarmed. "Hey – how do you know my name?"

"Never mind that. Just do it."

So he did, but very, very quickly and with his eyes closed.

"All right," said Gretl. "I suppose that will do."

Luckily, it did.

Aurora Rose opened her eyes for the first time in a hundred years and came face to face with Luke. What a horrible shock! She'd been dreaming about a tall, dark, and handsome prince. Instead she saw a very ordinary-looking boy with a

dirty face and a head of wild, curly brown hair, wearing weird clothes (jeans, sneakers, and a T-shirt). She started to scream.

Gretl leaned forward and gave her a poke in the ribs.

"Stop it at once," she snapped. "You're awake, aren't you? If it weren't for Luke, you would have slept forever. Imagine that."

Aurora sniffed and looked at Luke sideways from under her eyelashes. He was fidgeting. He always did that when he was embarrassed.

"Okay," he said. "I've kissed her. She's woken up. Now I'm going home."

"Not unless you take Aurora with you."

Luke looked at Gretl in disbelief.

"There is no way," he said firmly, "I'm taking a *girl* home. Come on! What would my mom say?"

"Well, there is absolutely no way," said Aurora quickly, "that I'd go anywhere with *him*. I never go anywhere without Ms. Wibberley as a chaperone."

"What's a chaperone?" asked Luke.

"Don't you even know *that*?" said Aurora. "She's someone who makes sure that you're never, *ever* alone with a young man. Especially if he comes from an unsuitable social background."

"Unsuitable social background?" repeated Luke. He had no idea at all what she was talking about.

"You don't need to worry about that anymore," said Gretl. "Things are much more relaxed these days. Too relaxed if you ask me. Anyway, dear Ms. Wibberley ran off just before you pricked your finger. She didn't like the idea of a hundred-year sleep. As for your mother and father, they were on a six-month vacation in the south of France. They missed everything. Never mind that their only daughter needed them at home. They always were a selfish couple. Still, no use crying over spilled milk."

"I don't believe you," said Aurora, her voice suddenly shaky. "You're making it up."

Luke looked horrified. "It would be a really terrible thing to have made up," he said, clenching his hands.

Gretl looked at Luke in surprise. Maybe he wasn't such a thoughtless little twerp after all.

"You're right," she said gently, "it would have been, but I'm afraid it's the truth."

At this point, Gretl decided she had to get a grip on herself. The last time she had gotten emotionally involved in a case, well... She shuddered. She only had to catch a glimpse of a piece of gingerbread and she started feeling uneasy.

"Is your mother at home, Luke?" Gretl asked, pulling herself together.

"Yes," said Luke. "She's going to be really worried about me. I only went out to get some milk and I've been gone for hours."

"There you are then," said Gretl to Aurora. "As you have neither parents nor governess, Luke's mother can act as a chaperone."

"I don't think..." Luke started to say, but then he stopped.

Most parents would run a mile at the thought of taking in a complete stranger, but Luke's mom wasn't like most parents. The *more* friends he brought home, the happier she was. She said it made the house feel warm and lived-in. So maybe she wouldn't think twice about taking a poor orphaned friend of his under her wing. Would she?

4

The Promise

"I've got one of those on my new safety cycle," said Aurora, looking at Luke's mountain bike, which was still lying on the grass outside the castle. She was pointing at the gearshift.

"The Victorians didn't have bikes with gears," said Luke quickly, hoping she wasn't going to ask him how they worked.

"Of course we did," she said scathingly. "They're very useful on hills." She paused for a second and then she said, "Is it terribly hilly where your castle is?"

Luke thought about 1223 Willow Street.

"No," he said, "and I don't live in a castle. I live in a three-bedroom ranch house."

"Goodness," said Aurora. "Only three bedrooms! Where on earth do all your servants sleep?"

Oh dear, thought Luke. He never answered questions at school if he could help it. Now it looked as if he was going to have to answer quite a few. He was about to start explaining, when Gretl came out of the castle.

"I've left Cook in charge," she said. "I told her you'll be back as soon as you've figured out a few things."

"What kind of things?" asked Aurora suspiciously. Everything had always been figured out for her.

"For starters, the twenty-first century," said Gretl, briskly.

At first, Aurora would not get on the handlebars of Luke's bicycle.

"You'll see my legs," she said.

Luke couldn't see how. She was wearing a long skirt, striped cotton stockings, and little black button-up boots.

"I couldn't care less about that," he said. "I'm more worried about something getting trapped in the wheels. That's if I can even ride with you on the bike too."

"Perhaps we should take our motor car instead," suggested Aurora.

"Great," said Luke, "as long as my bike will fit in the back. What kind of car is it, and who's going to drive?"

"It's the very latest model," said Aurora. "Normally Father drives. He used to make Williams, our chauffeur, walk in front with the red flag. Poor Williams. Sometimes he had to run because Papa drives terribly fast."

"Williams must be a very quick runner," said Luke, looking impressed.

"Oh, he is," said Aurora, nodding in agreement. "Papa never drives less than four miles an hour!"

"Mom got a speeding ticket once," said Luke. "She was doing eighty on the highway. I told her to slow down, but she didn't listen."

"Don't be silly," said Aurora snottily. "No one could possibly drive that fast. It wouldn't be safe. I suppose you mean *eight* miles an hour, but I still don't believe you."

Luke opened his mouth to argue, but what was the point? She'd find out soon enough about cars and highways and traffic. He almost felt sorry for her. Almost, but not quite. A little bit of him was looking forward to bragging about how much better things were these days. (Well, they are, aren't they?)

As it happened, they couldn't use the car. Ms. Wibberley and Williams the chauffeur had run away in it. They couldn't use Luke's bike, either. With Aurora on board, Luke couldn't get it to move.

"It's no use," he said. "We won't make it. Anyway, I think you'd better stay here until I've explained things to my mom. I'll come back and get you tomorrow."

"Promise!" said Aurora dramatically. "Because, apart from the castle servants and Gretl, you're the only person I know in the whole wide world. Everyone else is dead!"

Luke squirmed. He didn't want to be the only person she knew in the whole wide world. It sounded like a big responsibility, and so far, the only thing he'd ever been responsible for was cleaning his hamster's cage (and sometimes he forgot to do that).

"Well," he said, desperately looking for a way out, "I don't mean to sound rude or anything, but..."

"Promise you'll come back," said Gretl, "or I'll turn you into a..."

"Worm," said Luke miserably.

"Exactly," said Gretl. "Then I'll use you on my next fishing trip."

"Ooh," squealed Aurora, "how disgusting."

"All right, I *promise* I'll be back," said Luke. It didn't look as if he had much choice. Besides, it wasn't every day that you got to meet a real live Victorian, and he was also beginning to feel sort of sorry for her – even if she was irritating and bossy.

"All right," said Gretl. "Cutforth doesn't have phones, so I'll give you the number of my cell phone. Now, hop to it. Out of the castle gates, first left, and you'll be home in no time."

And he was.

5

Home for Supper

"What took you so long?" said Luke's mom.
"Hand me the milk, please. I'm dying for a
cup of coffee."

Oh, no, thought Luke, *I didn't get any!*

"Thanks," said his mom, picking up a
carton from the kitchen table. "Any change?"

Luke was amazed. Where had that milk
come from? It hadn't been there a minute
ago. He whirled around, expecting to see
Gretl standing close behind him.

"What's the matter?" asked his mom.
"What have you been up to?"

"Nothing," he said, fidgeting awkwardly.

It was as if Gretl still had a bony grip on his neck.

"Mom, um, there's something I need to tell you..."

Then (and this was the worst part), his mom came up and put her arm around him and gave him a big hug. "You know you can tell me anything, don't you?" she said in her most sugary voice.

"I met this girl," he said, still squirming, "on my way to the store."

"It's all right to talk to girls you know. They don't bite," said his mom. "So what's she like? Does she go to your school? Is she smart?"

"I don't know," said Luke, "but she's bossy. She made me promise I'll see her tomorrow."

"Are you going to?" asked Mrs. Lively, trying not to sound too interested.

"I'll have to," said Luke. "I promised that I would."

"Really?" Mrs. Lively was impressed. "So next time you promise to clean up your room, you'll do that too?"

Luke gave his mom a withering look.

"Where does this girl live, and does she have a name?"

"Cutforth Castle, and her name's Aurora." Luke's mom blinked.

"Cutforth *Castle?* Is it somewhere near here? I've never heard of it. Do her parents work there?"

"Uh, no. She doesn't have any parents," said Luke.

"How awful!" said Mrs. Lively. She didn't have a mom or dad either, and she missed them a lot. "Does she live with an aunt or something?"

"She has a sort of, um, godmother," said Luke, trying to sound as vague as possible.

He didn't really want to explain about Gretl Greta too.

"Why don't you give the poor girl a call and ask her if she'd like to come over for supper? We'll have pizza, fries, and chocolate ice cream."

Luke called Gretl's number.

"Hello," he said, when she answered. "I was wondering if Aurora..."

"Just a second," said Gretl, "I'll get her."

Aurora took the phone cautiously, as if she thought it might explode.

"AURORA ROSE RAMS-BOTHAM SPEAKING."

"It's me, Luke," he said, pulling the phone away from his ear. "You don't need to shout. I was just calling to see if you want to come over tomorrow.

Mom says she'll pick you up at five and take you home again later – if that's all right?"

He was desperately hoping it wouldn't be. He knew from studying the Victorians at school that they had all sorts of boring, complicated rules about mealtimes and visiting. He was expecting her to say something snotty, but she didn't. In fact, she sounded excited.

"What do you think we will we have for supper, Luke?"

"Pizza and fries," said Luke.

"Don't forget the chocolate ice cream," shouted his mom, who'd been listening in from the kitchen.

"How exotic," Aurora said. "Also, I can't wait to try some carbonated water with coloring, sulfite ammonia, caramel, sugar, phosphoric acid, sodium citrate, and citric acid."

"What's going on?" said the Minister, looking hard at Fickle's monitor. "How does she know about soda?"

"Gretl took her through the history of the last hundred years on her laptop."

"Excellent," said the Minister. "What did Aurora think of that?"

"The laptop? Oh, she said she'd read about it in the castle library. She then gave a very good description of Charles Babbage's design for a mechanical, programmable computer," Ron said, sounding impressed.

"No," snarled the Minister, "what did she think of the twenty-first century."

"She said, 'It sounds wonderful, but so does plain yogurt until you try it.'"

"I like plain yogurt," said the Minister. "We used to have it for breakfast when I was a small child."

"Horrible," said Ron.

Mrs. Lively liked to be on time, so they arrived at the castle early.

"My goodness," she exclaimed as she pulled up outside the gates. "Does Aurora really live here? I can't believe I haven't heard of this place before."

"It's never been open to the public," said Luke quickly.

"I don't think she'd mind if I took a peek," said Mrs. Lively.

She was just about to open her door, when Luke leaped from the car, saying, "Stay there, Mom. I don't think walking around a castle is a good idea. Not when you've had such a tiring day at work."

Mrs. Lively looked surprised. Luke never normally worried about how tired she was. Still, she didn't want to discourage him from being thoughtful, so she said, "Maybe you're right. I'll just listen to the radio while you go and get her." She gave him an encouraging smile, leaned back, and prepared to sing along with the radio.

Luke shot out of the car to find Aurora. He was in a hurry to get this over with.

Mrs. Lively was still singing when she saw Luke walking back toward her. What she saw made her sit up, blink, and rub her eyes. When she looked again, nothing had changed.

Luke had a girl with him – a girl wearing a hat, lace gloves, striped stockings, black button-up boots, and carrying a velvet purse and a parasol.

How unusual, thought Mrs. Lively, somewhat puzzled, but she gave them a friendly wave anyway.

She still looked confused when Luke and Aurora reached the car.

"I'll sit in front," said Luke, rushing to open the front passenger door. "You can get in the back."

Aurora wasn't used to being told what to do.

"I always sit next to Father when he drives. You may sit in the back, Luke," she said.

Mrs. Lively gave her a warm smile as she got in the front passenger seat.

"I'm Luke's mom," she said, "and you must be Aurora."

"Aurora Rose Rams-Botham," said Aurora a little stiffly. "I am very pleased to meet you."

"Well, Aurora Rose Rams-Botham, I'm very pleased to meet you too. That's a lovely straw hat you're wearing," said Mrs. Lively, leaning over and snapping Aurora's seat belt in place. "However, you'll have to take it off, or you'll block my view."

Normally, Luke's mom enjoyed cruising around in the car, but having Aurora in the passenger seat was like driving with a very young and incredibly nosy child. She wanted to touch everything and couldn't sit still for a second.

"Ooh," she squealed excitedly as she pushed a button and the electric windows flew up and down. "How do they do that? What does this do?"

"NO!" screeched Luke's mom as Aurora grabbed and yanked up the emergency brake.

There was a strong smell of burning rubber from the tires, and the car slid to a halt.

"Now, Aurora," said Mrs. Lively. "I want you to sit tight on your hands until we get home. Do you understand?"

Aurora nodded. "I..."

Luke's mom gave her a stern look.

They drove home in total silence, even when Luke's mom swerved to avoid a car whose driver wasn't watching the road. Luke was impressed. Aurora turned a deep green color, but she didn't move a muscle. Then, when they got home, she opened the car door, got out, and promptly fainted.

Luke had to help his mom carry her inside the house.

"Fan her with the newspaper," his mom said. "I'll try to get her boots off."

"Good grief!" Mrs. Lively said a moment later. "No wonder the poor girl passed out. She must be suffocating in all these clothes. Look, she's even wearing petticoats and every last thing has been hand stitched."

Mrs. Lively picked up Aurora's velvet purse and looked at it very closely. "I don't believe this – there's even a monogram embroidered on her purse.

"There are two rams and some sort of a motto. It's written so small I can hardly read it. What does it say: *Fear not the Sheep*? Oh, silly me, it's *Fear not the Sleep*. How strange! You know, the last time I saw clothes like these was in a museum. I'd give anything to know where she got them."

"I don't think," Luke said carefully, "that the store is still in business."

6

Why Can't She Go Somewhere Else?

"More fries?" asked Luke's mom with an approving smile. It was nice to see a girl with such a healthy appetite.

"Yes, please, Mrs. Lively!" said Aurora. "*And* pizza. And soda. And ketchup. Then I would like some chocolate ice cream and some of that squirty cream out of a can. If you have some, I would very much like to try potato chips. I'm most terribly hungry. It seems like forever since I had anything to eat, and you're such a wonderful cook."

"Huh," snorted Luke. His mom, a wonderful cook? Still, he couldn't help watching in fascination as Aurora devoured more pizza, demolished three bowls of ice cream, and plowed through half a bag of potato chips.

When it looked as though she'd finally finished eating, Mrs. Lively said, "Okay, kids, I've got some work to do. Luke, you can clear the table, and I'd like a cup of coffee, please. Oh, sweetie, remember – not too much milk."

Luke made a face.

"Don't worry, Mrs. Lively," Aurora said sweetly. "I shall ring for the maid to bring your coffee to you."

Luke's mom laughed. They could still hear her laughing as she walked to the front room.

"Did I say something amusing?" asked Aurora seriously.

"We don't *have* a maid," said Luke. "People don't have them anymore. At least, not unless they've got tons of money – which we definitely don't."

"Oh," said Aurora. "So... who does all the work around your home?"

Luke didn't know where to start explaining, so he simply pointed to the pile of plates on the kitchen table and said, "The dishwasher will do those."

"Dishwasher?" said Aurora. "I thought you said you didn't have any servants."

"No! It's that white thing over there." He nodded carelessly in the direction of the sink. "You load it up, and I'll take Mom a cup of hot coffee."

When he came back, Aurora had just loaded the washing machine with dirty plates, knives, and forks.

"Simple!" she said, slamming the door and pressing the extra-fast spin button. She turned to Luke with a big smile. "What happens next?"

As soon as she heard the sound of her best china being smashed into thousands of tiny pieces, Luke's mom came running. "What on earth...?"

She leaped forward and unplugged the machine. Then she bent down and looked inside it. She straightened up slowly.

"Now," she said, "tell me what's going on around here. I want to know why Aurora's dressed up like a Victorian girl, what happened to her parents, and why she just loaded my washing machine full of dishes. Luke, this had better be good."

"Oh dear," said the Minister, picking up the phone. "This is going to be tricky. Gretl!" he bellowed into the mouthpiece. "I want you at Luke's house immediately!"

"Don't worry," said Ron soothingly. "Mrs. Lively won't believe a word they tell her."

The Minister looked doubtful, but Ron was right. She didn't.

"I stopped believing in fairy tales years ago," snapped Mrs. Lively. "So stop messing around. I'll count to ten, Luke. If you haven't told me the truth by then, I'll..."

"Turn him into a worm."

Luke felt Gretl's bony grip on his shoulder.

"Just joking!" said Gretl, stepping forward and shaking Mrs. Lively's hand. "I'm Aurora's godmother and you must be Luke's mom. I hope you don't mind me dropping in like this. You must be wondering why Aurora's a little unusual."

"I am not," squealed Aurora.

"I was wondering that," said Mrs. Lively.

"It's like this..." said Gretl, lowering her voice and placing a hand confidingly on Mrs. Lively's arm. Luke's mom hurried her off into the living room.

"I wonder what Gretl's telling her?" said Luke. He and Aurora were in the kitchen.

"I'll bet she's making up some tragic story about my parents taking off abroad, leaving me to be brought up by a crazy governess."

"Mom will definitely fall for it," said Luke.

"You can't blame her for not believing our story, can you? I'm having the most awful trouble believing it myself."

"What exactly did happen?" asked Luke.

She was silent so he tried again. "Did you prick your finger on a spinning wheel, like it says in the story?"

"No," Aurora said in her snotty tone. "Of course not. It was a sewing machine, silly. I was taking it apart to see how it worked."

Aurora was just about to give Luke a detailed account when Mrs. Lively and Gretl came back looking pleased with themselves.

"Gretl thinks you need to be in school full-time as soon as possible, Aurora, and I agree with her. It's not good for a girl of your age to be drifting around in fancy clothes."

"We've been in touch with the school district," said Gretl. "Once I explained things, they said that you could go to Luke's school right away."

"Luke's school?" said Aurora. "I don't think I should feel comfortable at a *boys'* school."

"Mixed," said Mrs. Lively. "Boys *and* girls."

"Goodness," said Aurora. "How modern that sounds. I suppose the girls have to study things like sewing and drawing and music.

Then the lucky boys get to study science and mathematics and athletics."

"We all get to do everything," said Luke. "Unfortunately."

"Everything?" breathed Aurora. She could hardly believe her luck. "Even experiments and blowing things up and taking things apart?"

"Um – of course," said Mrs. Lively. "Well, otherwise it wouldn't be fair, would it?"

"Mom," said Luke.

They were straightening up the guest room so that Aurora could move in.

"What?" said Mrs. Lively.

She looked cheerful. There was nothing she liked more than a challenge, and Aurora was challenging indeed. She just couldn't get over the things that girl said and did!

Mrs. Lively figured that if you didn't know better, you'd be forgiven for thinking modern-day life had simply passed Aurora by.

"Does Aurora *have* to go to my school?" said Luke. "It's not fair. Why can't she go somewhere else? Also, why does she have to come and stay here?"

"Why, Luke, I thought you'd like to help the poor girl. Imagine *me* going off and leaving you all alone in the house to take care of everything. Think how *you'd* feel." She was tucking in the sheets on the spare bed, so she couldn't see Luke's face.

"Aurora's godmother is very eager for her to go to school with you. She told me all about Aurora's unusual upbringing. You're the first real friend she's ever had. Amazing, isn't it?"

Luke's mom shook her head. "As for staying here, she can't walk to school from the castle, can she? It's too far, and there's no school bus, and no one at the castle can drive. So, unless you have a better idea..."

He didn't, but he tried to argue anyway, even though he knew arguing with his logical mom was impossible. "She won't know anything, and she's so old-fashioned! You know how the kids are – everyone will pick on her, and then they'll pick on me too. It'll be a huge disaster, Mom."

"Once she's in her school uniform, she'll look just like everyone else. You'll see," Luke's mom said firmly.

And that was that.

7

The Favor

"There's no way I'm walking in with you
looking like that. Everyone will laugh," said
Luke, hovering outside the classroom door.
Of the 260 girls at Luke's school, only Aurora
was wearing a long black skirt, lace gloves,
and a straw hat as part of the uniform.

"They wouldn't dare," said Aurora. She sounded very confident, and there was a determined glint in her eye. She grasped the doorknob firmly and swept into the classroom, with Luke trailing behind. There were a couple of giggles and someone snickered.

They soon stopped when Ms. Humperdink, Luke's terrifying teacher, found herself starting to curtsy. *How bizarre,* she thought, as she felt her knees bend and her head dip.

Aurora smiled graciously and introduced herself.

"I will sit here," she said, taking Ms. Humperdink's chair and pulling it up to the teacher's desk.

Luke let out a strangled gasp. You could have heard a pip squeak, as the class looked first at Aurora and then at their teacher.

"You have to admit," said Luke's friend
Winston, as they lined up for lunch, "it was a
totally impressive thing to do. I can't believe
old Humperdink just let her do it!"

"My mom says she has natural authority,"
said Luke.

They turned to look at Aurora, who was
surrounded by an admiring group of girls.

"Mom got her a uniform, but she wouldn't
even try it on – except for the tie. She said
there just wasn't enough of it and she'd feel
undressed!"

"Not enough uniform. That's weird," said Winston. "Most of the girls here think there's way too much."

They sat in silence for a minute. Then Luke said, "She's used to wearing layers of clothes. I mean, suppose someone tried to make you go to school wearing only pants."

"I'd like to see them try," said Winston.

"So would I," said Luke.

"Good grief," said Mrs. Lively as they were having a snack after school. "Did you really sit at Ms. Humperdink's desk, Aurora?"

"It was the only one available," Aurora answered absently. She was glued to the TV. She had the remote control in her hand, and she kept changing channels and turning the sound up and down.

"Don't do that, Aurora," said Mrs. Lively, "or you'll break it."

Aurora said, "Oh, sorry." Then she discovered the TV Internet connection.

"This is so wonderful. You have no idea!"

"That's nothing compared to what she did at school, Mom," said Luke. "She sent an e-mail to the president and said that her father was a good friend of his. She actually expected a response, right then and there! Isn't that crazy?"

"A friend of the president?" said Mrs. Lively. "How interesting."

At school, Aurora was making quite a reputation for herself. It had been a long time since the teachers had taught anyone who was so eager to learn. She wanted to know how *everything* worked. If no one could explain, she would take things apart and find out for herself. Aurora was a hit with the girls too. They'd even started dressing like her.

"Amazing," said Ron.

The Minister nodded in admiration.

"Things have turned out much better than we could have hoped. Not the traditional ending we've been used to, of course, but perfectly acceptable in this day and age."

"It's more interesting too," said Ron. "I can't wait to find out what happens next."

"More interesting, perhaps," said Gretl, who was back at H.Q., "but there are still some loose ends that need to be tied up."

"What kind of loose ends?" asked the Minister nervously.

"I know that Mother and Father were in the south of France, and Williams and Ms. Wibberley ran off before the Big Sleep," said Gretl, "but two hundred castle servants have just woken up to find they're a hundred years behind the times. Have you thought about what's going to happen to them?"

"Um," said the Minister, looking more and more uncomfortable. "It hasn't ever been a problem before."

"Two hundred Victorians. What can they do at the beginning of the twenty-first century that will pay their wages *and* keep people from asking awkward questions?"

"I have no idea," said Ron cheerfully.

The Minister looked blank.

"You can't think of anything?" said Gretl. "It's a good thing I'm still on the case.

Richard Whittington owes me a favor. Let's see what he can do for us."

"What kind of favor?" asked the Minister suspiciously.

"Who do you think sold him the cat?" said Gretl.

8

Ride On!

A few days later, Luke's mom was reading a letter from school about a trip to Trentham Towers, the best theme park around.

"I'd love to go," said Aurora. "I haven't been to Trentham Towers for years. We spent every Christmas there when I was little."

"It's *very* expensive. I don't..."

"Come on, Mom," said Luke, "we've got to go. It's research. We need to design a theme park for our information technology unit. The best one gets entered in a competition sponsored by Richard Whittington. You know, the pest control billionaire who has a silver rat on the hood of his Jaguar? The first prize is ten state-of-the-art computers for our school."

"Well, the school could certainly use those," said Mrs. Lively. "If you're that excited about it, I guess you'd better go."

"Does Aurora know that the present-day Duke has turned Trentham Towers into a theme park?" asked the Minister.

"No," said Ron.

"Ah," said the Minister.

Aurora was peering out of the bus window.

"What are those people doing?"

"They're lining up to pay," explained Luke.

"PAY?" screeched Aurora. "You mean the Duke makes people pay to get in?"

"Of course he does," said Luke. "He needs the money."

"What on earth for?"

"He has to pay people's wages, and fix stuff, and pay taxes – just like you need money to keep Cutforth Castle running. Unless you're going to sell it, of course."

"SELL CUTFORTH CASTLE?" yelled Aurora. "Of course I'm not. What a stupid idea."

"Then I sure hope you have lots of cash," said Luke.

"I certainly do," said Aurora, wondering what cash was and where she could get some.

"Does she?" Ron asked the Minister.

"Unfortunately not," he replied. "Prince Hugo was the one with all the money."

Ron let out a long, low whistle. "Shivering shingles!"

"Why is that woman wearing such silly clothes?" Aurora demanded as a Queen Elizabeth the First look-alike strolled past them casually.

"Trentham Towers is a theme park," Luke explained patiently. "It's supposed to be set in Elizabethan times."

"Are you telling me that people actually pay to see this sort of thing?"

"Yes, but there are rides as well. Most people come to go on those."

"Rides?" asked Aurora. "What kind of rides?"

9

Wait and See

Aurora was watching the corkscrewing
Dangle of Death with total concentration.
Then she said, "How will I keep my hat on
when we're hanging upside down?"

"I'll hold it for you while you go on the
ride," said Luke.

"Oh, Luke, don't be silly," she said,
marching him right to the front of the line.

(No one complained. They thought she was part of the show.) "You're coming with me. We have to experience *everything*, or we won't be able to design our own park."

"We?" said Luke. "Who said I was going to be your project partner?"

"It's up to you," she said, fastening herself firmly into one of the ride's seats, "but I've got a great idea that will win us that prize – an idea that will mean I'll never have to sell Cutforth and move away."

Luke almost said, "I wouldn't mind if you did move," but the words just didn't come out. Just think: no more waiting to use the bathroom. No more having to share his computer. No more public embarrassment when Aurora got all excited about escalators, supermarkets, skateboards, and neon signs. Still, he thought he *might* miss her. Life had been a little less dull since she'd moved in.

"All right, all right," he said grudgingly, "but don't blame me if speeding upside down at sixty miles an hour makes me sick."

Luke's stomach had never done very well on amusement park rides.

By the time they got home, Luke was worn out. Aurora had made him try each ride at least twice and they'd sat through three different shows.

"Raiders of the Lost Potatoes was awesome," said Aurora. She was standing in the kitchen eating a bag of chips.

"The part where Sir Walter Raleigh stole the potatoes right out from under the noses of those pirates was cool. Who knew potatoes could be so exciting?" said Luke.

Aurora nodded. "We can have the same kind of thing in Victorian World, only not with potatoes."

"Victorian World?"

"Our theme park," said Aurora.

"No way," said Luke. "We'll never win the prize with such a boring idea."

"It won't be boring at all," said Aurora crossly. "Why does everyone think the Victorians are boring? Look at all the exploring and inventing we did. Wait and see. It won't be boring at all."

Luke had been waiting for days, but Aurora wouldn't show him what she was doing.

"It's my project too," he complained. He was just about to start banging on the guest-room door, when she came out looking pleased with herself.

"There," she said, handing Luke a beautiful water-color painting of Victorian World.

"It's awesome. Very artistic," said Luke.

"Look," she said. "Here is Cutforth Castle right in the middle. I thought we'd open it to the public. We won't even have to get the staff to pretend to be Victorian! Outside we'll have the Victoria Falls Flume. That will be part of Dr. Livingstone's African Adventure. Then I thought we'd have Carroll's Wild Ride, Dickens' World, Edison's Electric Emporium, Grimaldi's Big Top..."

"But..."

"What?"

"This will look great on the Victorian World brochure, but we also need an actual design, with each ride drawn accurately."

Luke smiled at her so she wouldn't get mad at his suggestion. "Come look at my theme park game on the computer. Once we've taken a good look at the castle, we can customize it and print out a real plan. Your drawing on the front, and my plan inside."

"*Our* plan," said Aurora firmly. "I shall be asking the Head Gardener for his detailed map of the castle grounds. He's measured every inch of the estate already."

"Great," said Luke. "That will save a lot of work. Remember, though, there's still tons to be done and only a few weeks to do it."

10

Winner Takes All

"That's it," said Aurora, as they handed in their theme park competition entry. "We've done the best we can."

"You certainly have," said Mrs. Lively.

She was impressed. She had never seen Luke work so hard on anything before. The last two weeks had been blissful. He hadn't grumbled once about being bored.

She was a little worried about her phone bill, though. The kids seemed to have spent a lot of time making long-distance calls and sending faxes to firms with names like Batty's Engineering, Theme Dream, and Rides R Us.

Their work had paid off. When they showed her the finished project, she was amazed at all the detail they had put into it.

"How on earth did you manage to put this together?" she gasped. "You even found out how much it would cost!" She thought the only thing Luke knew about money was how to spend it.

"Oh, that was easy," said Aurora. "It's amazing what information people are willing to share. That nice woman at Trentham Towers was really helpful."

"I think you deserve to win. I really do," said Mrs. Lively, giving them both a big kiss. "If that Richard Whittington's got any sense, he'll think so too."

"Of course he will," said the Minister. "He will, won't he?"

"Probably," said Gretl. "He's an excellent businessperson. As soon as I mentioned Cutforth Castle, he began to see the possibilities. I could almost see the dollar signs flashing in front of his eyes."

"Then he'll give them the prize. Besides, I thought he owed you a favor."

"He did, but he paid that back by setting up the competition. He made me agree that Aurora and Luke would only win if they deserved to. He said he has his reputation to consider. I guess there's a first time for everything!" she said.

"Anyway" Gretl continued slyly, "I think you'll find that they do win. She's a bright young lady and Luke isn't quite the total loss I thought he was going to be. They work well together. I just had to nudge things along in the right direction. Didn't take much – a phone call here, a word there. Nothing any other godmother wouldn't do."

Meanwhile, at Finney Hall, where the Awards Ceremony was about to take place, Richard Whittington was feeling jittery.

He'd been feeling jittery ever since Gretl had started him on the idea of theme parks. He knew this was his chance to make a fortune, but would Gretl tell everyone he was trying to make money from something dreamed up by kids? Had she seen through him somehow?

He broke out in a cold sweat every time the competition was mentioned.

Actually, this happened fairly often, because the press had heard rumors that he was planning to branch out of pest control and into leisure management.

"Was Richard Whittington hoping to use the winning competition entry as a blueprint for a new theme park?" they kept asking. "If so, does he have a site in mind?"

At last he saw the winning entry. He'd been careful not to judge the competition himself. He had a whole committee to blame if things went wrong. Still, as it happened, he didn't have to worry. He rubbed his hands together with glee.

Luke and Aurora's entry had been magnificently thought out. It was a clear winner – and now he could think about making it a reality.

"Cutforth Castle," sighed Richard happily. "What a dream of a place! It's miles from anywhere, but close to everything!"

All he had to do now was talk terms with the castle's owner. She was only a young girl, so there couldn't be any problems. His lawyers would have the contract drawn up and signed in no time.

He stepped up to the microphone, with a big white envelope in one hand.

"I won't feel happy until we know who's won," said the Minister, who was watching the Awards Ceremony live on Fickle's monitor.

Gretl didn't say anything, but she wouldn't feel happy either.

"And the winner is… Aurora Rams-Botham and Luke Lively of Maple School. Let's give them a big round of applause, ladies and gentlemen."

Aurora and Luke were quickly propelled onstage.

"Also…" Richard held up his hand for silence, "I'd like to make another announcement. As long as Ms. Rams-Botham and I can make a deal – and I'm sure we can – I'm planning to open a real Victorian World at Cutforth Castle this time next year."

"That's *wonderful!*" Luke whispered to Aurora, who was standing right next to him. "Imagine! All our rides in action. We never thought you'd be able to afford to do that."

Strangely enough, Aurora did not look pleased. She was about to speak, when something totally unexpected happened.

"Good grief!" gasped the Minister. "What on earth is *he* doing here?"

"Who?" asked Ron, peering hard at Fickle's monitor.

"Don't you recognize him? It's Prince Hugo! I thought he was eloping with his Personal Fitness Trainer."

"He almost did," said Ron, "but his father threatened to cut him off without a penny, so he dropped Paula like a hot potato."

"Serves him right," said the Minister.

"I hope he isn't going to mess things up," said Gretl.

"What do you mean?" asked the Minister.

"Prince Hugo is very good looking," said Gretl quickly.

"Yes, but he's such a rotten person," said Ron indignantly. "She wouldn't choose him instead of Luke, would she?"

"We'll have to wait and see," said Gretl. "Won't we?"

By this time, dark and handsome Prince Hugo was on stage and down on one knee in front of Aurora.

"Ooh," gasped the audience. Things were getting *really* interesting.

"Cast aside this weak and puny excuse for a prince," exclaimed Prince Hugo, sneering at Luke. "Let me whisk you away to a new life."

"Aah," sighed the audience. This was more like it.

"Certainly not," said Aurora.

"But I'm Hugo. Don't you know who I am?"

Aurora looked annoyed. She did know who he was. He was the dark and handsome prince of her dreams – the one who should have woken her up with a kiss.

As it was, Luke had done it instead. She glanced across at him. He was fidgeting like crazy, looking even more uncomfortable than normal. He really was a pretty great guy.

"I don't want a new life," she said, scowling at Hugo. "Now that I'm into it, I'm really enjoying this one."

Then something occurred to her. "I bet the only reason you're here is because you think I'm going to sell Cutforth Castle to Richard Whittington for millions of dollars."

Richard beamed and nodded approvingly.

"Well, I'm not."

Richard stopped beaming.

"At least Luke's not after my money. So you can beat it, Hugo – I don't need you."

"We're supposed to live happily ever after, though. It says so in all the books," whined Prince Hugo.

"This is the twenty-first century for goodness' sake," said Aurora. "I don't intend to get married for years, and when I do decide to, I don't intend to choose a husband from a book.

"By the way," she said, turning to Richard, "if you still want to talk about Victorian World, you can send me a fax tomorrow at Luke's house."

"Oh," said Luke, still fidgeting, "so you're still staying with us?"

"Of course," said Aurora. "As long as you don't mind, that is."

"Oh, I guess I don't," said Luke, trying to sound casual.

"I'm going to need a lot of help," she said.

"With what?" asked Luke.

"Victorian World. I'm not going to let Richard Whittington take over the whole thing. It will have to be a three-way partnership. That way, we'll always be able to out-vote him."

"A three-way partnership?" asked Luke.

"Me, you, and Richard. You *are* going to be my partner, aren't you?"

"Of course!" said Luke. "Does that mean I'll get paid?"

"Maybe," said Aurora, "but only if you help me with something else."

"What?" asked Luke, suddenly suspicious.

"History homework," said Aurora looking very serious. "I'm very good up until 1895. After that it's more or less a complete blank. Have I missed much?"

"Well, let's see... Two world wars," said Luke airily, "women getting the vote, humans landing on the moon... and that's just for starters."

"Excellent," said the Minister as they watched Luke and Aurora wander off in search of Luke's mom.

Mrs. Lively had heard that Richard Whittington was looking for a new accountant, so she was waiting for him offstage.

The Minister turned off the monitor and sat back. "Well, we have a happy ending after all. We won't have to worry about the next Sleeping Beauty for a long time, either."

"No," said Gretl "but I still have the Three Pigs to sort out."

"Really?" said the Minister. "I thought they were pretty straightforward."

"They were," sighed Gretl, "but these days people *want* to make houses out of wood and straw. It's a very ecological thing to do. So I think the tale needs a little tweak for the twenty-first century."

"Of course," said Ron.

About the Author

Fairy tales have fascinated me since I was knee-high to a wicked witch. Some of them made me anxious: *Snow White, The Snow Queen,* and *Hansel and Gretl.* Some of them made me smile and cheer: *Three Billy Goats Gruff, Three Little Pigs, Jack and the Beanstalk.*

All of them made me think, and one of them, *Sleeping Beauty,* made me think so hard, I decided to write my own version of it!

You see, there was one thing about the story I could *never* understand: Everyone in the castle goes to sleep for a hundred years and when they wake up, nothing's changed.

Really! I mean, how likely is *that?*

Debbie White